SPACE VOYAGE

VOYAGE THROUGH THE SOLAR SYSTEM

CATHERINE BARR

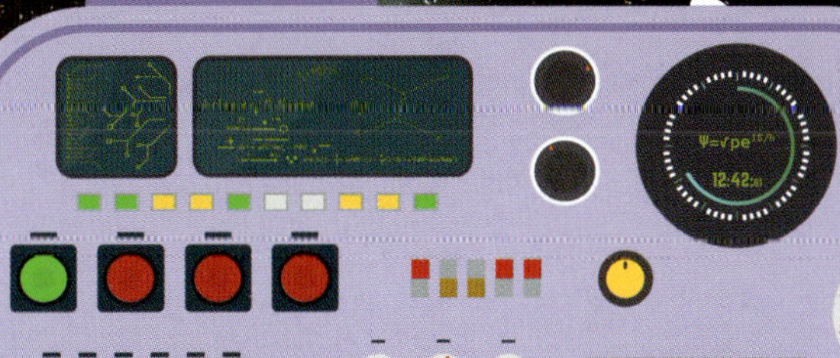

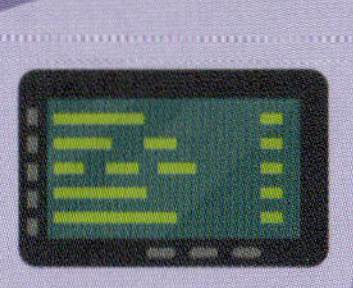

PowerKiDS press

Published in 2022 by The Rosen Publishing Group, Inc.
29 East 21st Street, New York, NY 10010

Originally Published in English by Haynes Publishing under the title:
Space Pocket Manual © Catherine Barr 2019

Cataloging-in-Publication Data

Names: Barr, Catherine.
Title: Voyage through the solar system / Catherine Barr.
Description: New York : PowerKids Press, 2022. | Series: Space voyage
Identifiers: ISBN 9781725331990 (pbk.) | ISBN 9781725332010 (library bound) | ISBN 9781725332003 (6 pack) | ISBN 9781725332027 (ebook)
Subjects: LCSH: Planets--Juvenile literature. | Solar system--Juvenile literature.
Classification: LCC QB501.3 B365 2022 | DDC 523.4--dc23

Design and layout by Richard Parsons

Photo Credits: Cover, p. 1 (control panel) Sky vectors/Shutterstock.com; cover, p. 1 (background) hideto999/Shutterstock.com; pp. 6-32 (background), 3 (background), 4-5 (background), 6 (bottom), 7 (both), 8 (bottom), 9 (top), 10, 11, 12 (bottom), 13 (top), 14, 15, 16-17 (background), 18-19 (background), 20-21 (background), 24 (top), 25, 26 (both), 27, 28 (both), 29 (both) Shutterstock.com; p. 8-9 (background), 12 (top), 13 (bottom), 17 (both), 18 (bottom), 21 (right), 22, 23 (both), 24 (bottom) Courtesy of NASA.

Manufactured in the United States of America

CPSIA Compliance Information: Batch #CSPK22. For Further Information contact Rosen Publishing, New York, New York at 1-800-237-9932.

CONTENTS

OUR SOLAR SYSTEM

In our galaxy alone, there are more than 2,500 stars with orbiting planets. Explore our own very special solar system...

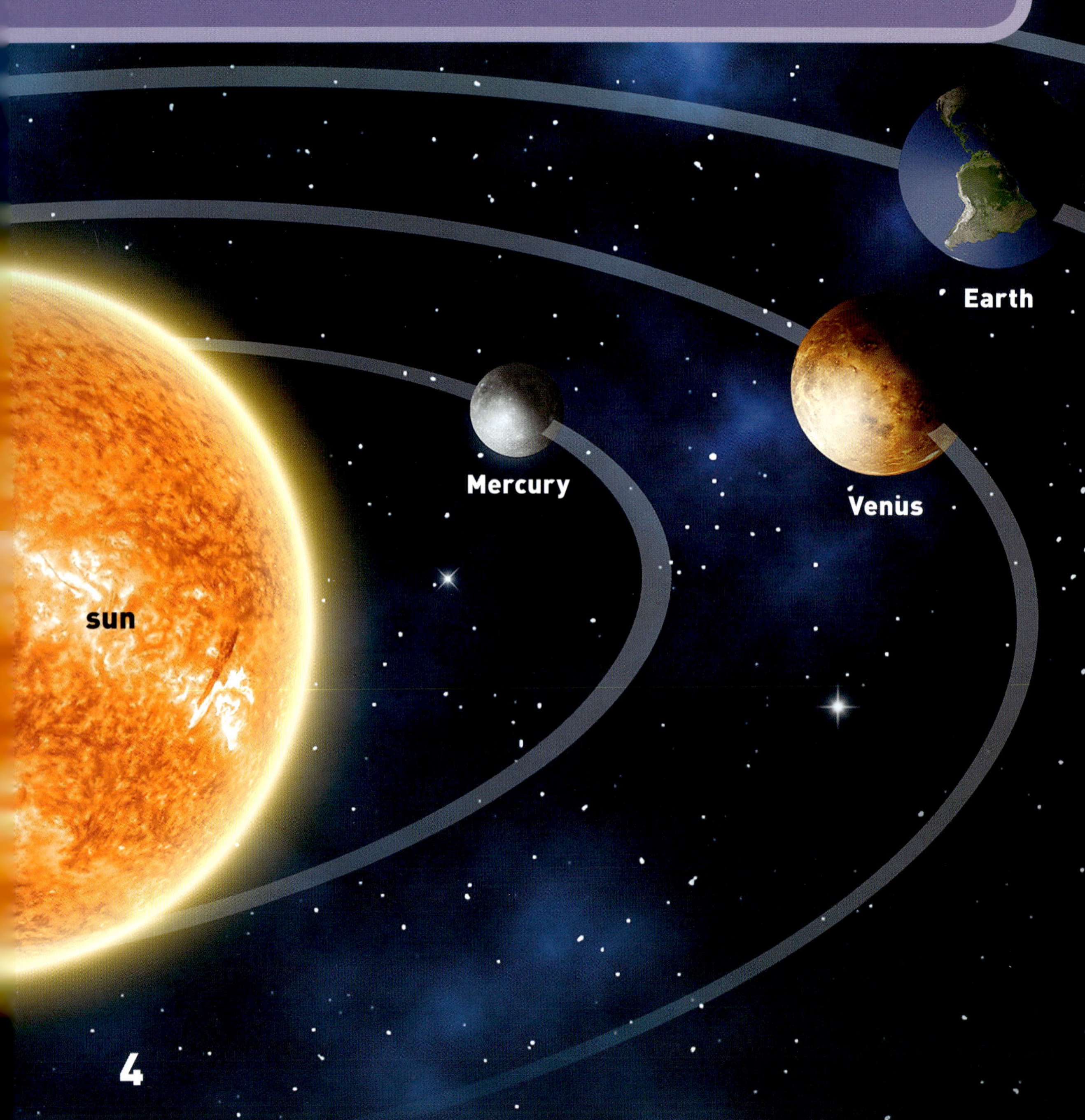

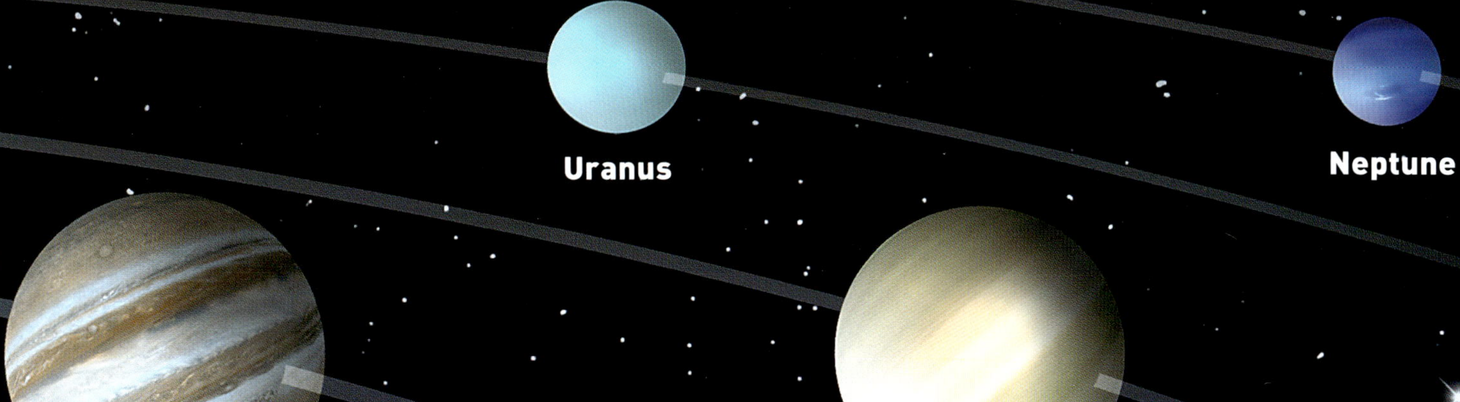

DID YOU KNOW?

Our solar system used to have nine planets, including an icy ball called Pluto. But in 2006, scientists voted, controversially, to knock Pluto off the planet list because it was too small. Pluto is still spinning beyond Neptune, but is now called a dwarf planet.

THE SPIN

1. GETTING STARTED

The solar system began with spinning clouds of dust and gas. Around 4.5 billion years ago, these clouds swirled so fast that they began to shine and our yellow sun was born.

2. THE PLANETS ARE CREATED

Leftover particles of dust and gas bumped and clumped together, eventually forming the four small rocky planets closest to the sun: Mercury, Venus, Earth, and Mars. Far away from the sun's warmth, four gigantic gas planets formed: Jupiter, Saturn, Uranus, and Neptune.

3. ASTEROIDS AND COMETS

Circling space rocks and ice eventually formed dwarf planets, moons, rings, asteroids, and comets orbiting the sun.

- Billions of potato-shaped space rocks make up a belt of asteroids spinning between Mars and Jupiter.
- Broken bits of asteroids and comets make up the spectacular rings of Saturn.
- Trillions of comets, or "dirty snowballs," fly towards the sun from the Oort Cloud, a ring of icy objects that scientists believe circles the far reaches of our solar system.

DID YOU KNOW?

Shooting stars are the streaks of light in the sky caused by space rocks called meteroids burning up as they enter Earth's atmosphere and become meteors.

A SPECIAL STAR

Our sun is 4.5 billion years old. It is a shining ball of gases that makes up 99.8 percent of the mass of the whole solar system. It is the sun that makes life possible here on Earth. Like every star, one day the sun will die. It is now halfway through its life. Humans may not be around, but in 5 billion years it will swell into a gigantic ball of red gas and engulf our solar system!

Sunspots

The sun's surface has shifting dark spots called sunspots. These darker patches are places where the surface is less hot than the overall scalding temperature of about 10,000°F (5,500°C).

Sunlight

It takes 8 minutes and 20 seconds for sunlight to reach Earth.

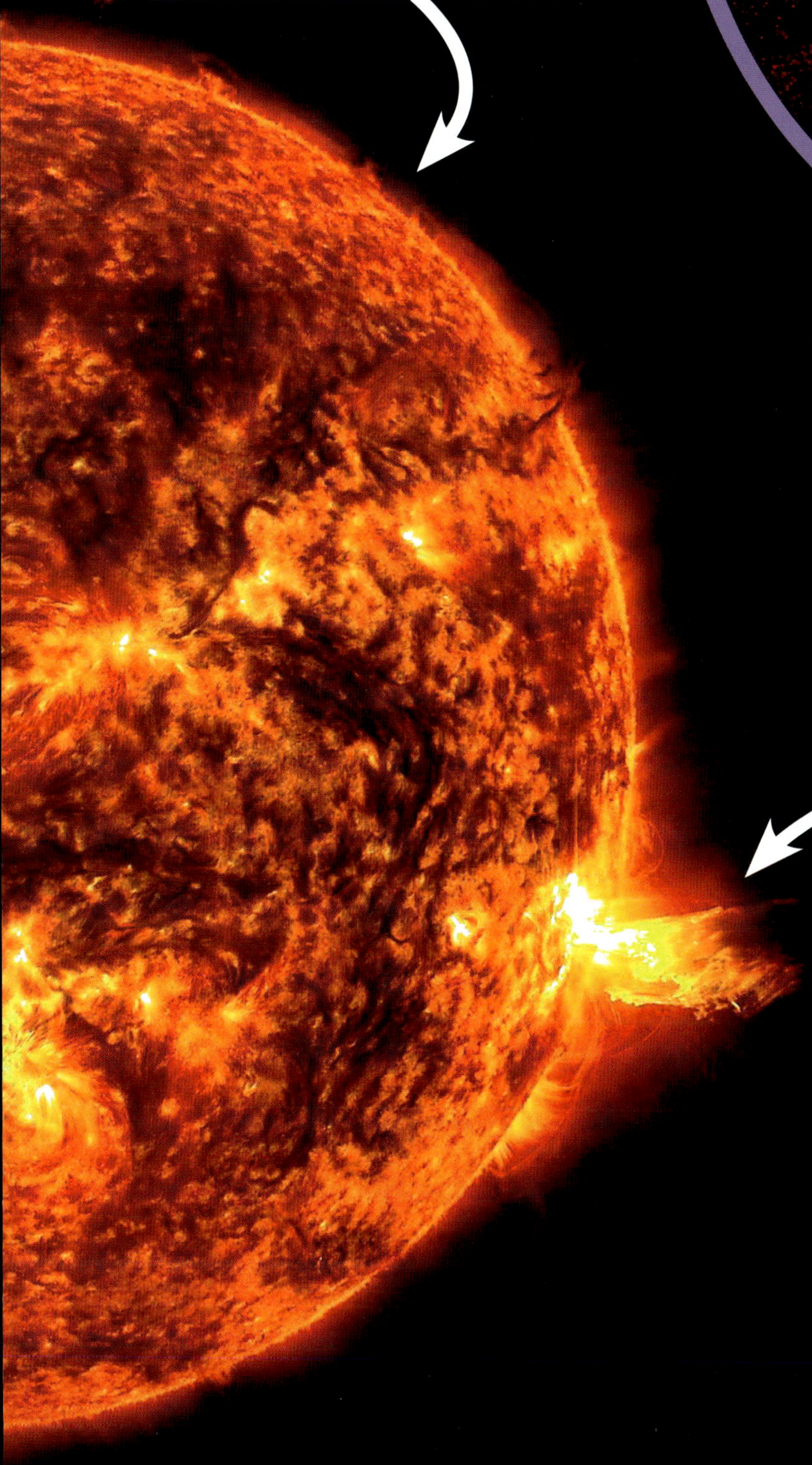

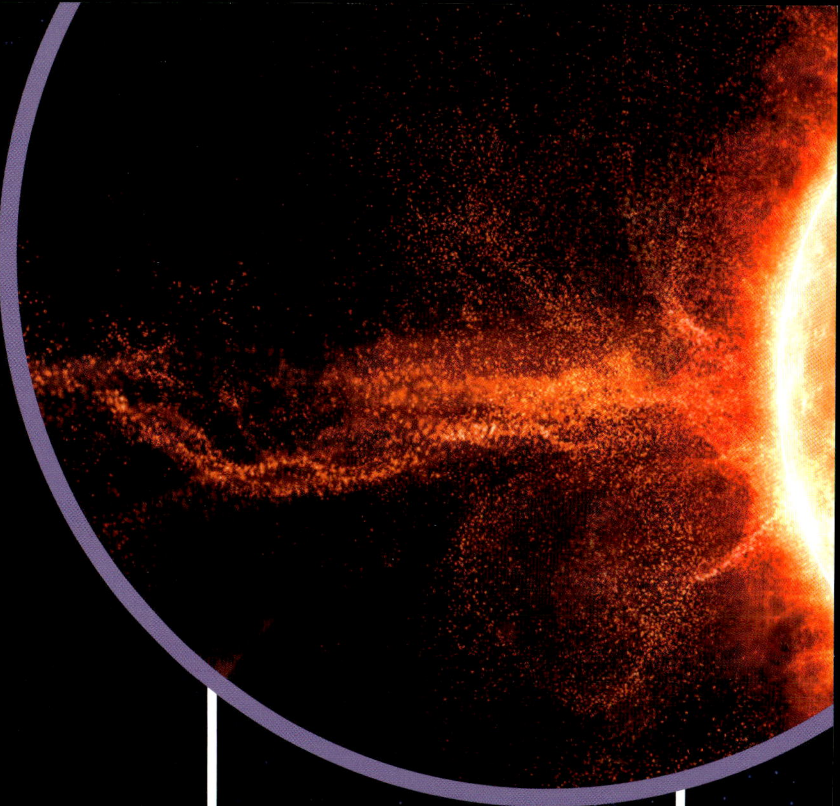

Solar Flares

Supersonic solar winds explode and loop out from the surface of the sun. The flashing curtains of northern and southern lights, called auroras, are caused by solar winds that reach Earth and clash with our planet's magnetic field. The auroras are seen where the magnetic field is strongest, toward the North and South Poles.

FOCUS ON THE PLANETS

Mercury "Swift Planet"

- Speedy orbit but a slower spin than Earth
- Burning hot in the day and freezing at night
- A dusty gray-brown surface of craters or "wrinkles"

Closest to the sun

Earth "Blue Planet"

- The only planet with water on its surface
- In the "Goldilocks zone;" the right amount of light and heat from the sun to support life

Venus "Morning Star"

- Scorching hot with a thick, choking atmosphere of clouds and acid rain
- Below the yellow clouds it has a black, barren surface of solid lava flows

Mars "Red Planet"

- Dry, dusty red surface with dust storms
- It has two moons
- Its Olympus Mons is three times as high as Mount Everest

Saturn "The Jewel"

- Giant gas planet with rings of rock and ice
- Has ferocious winds and storms
- Has 53 named moons. One, Titan, has the only atmosphere of any moon in the solar system.

Neptune "Big Blue"

- There may be an ocean of superhot water under its cold clouds
- Has supersonic winds

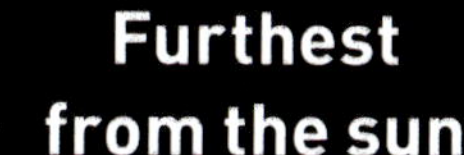
Furthest from the sun

Jupiter "Giant Planet"

- Monster hurricanes. The great red spot is a storm so big that Earth could fit inside it.
- It has 79 moons. Some have oceans beneath their crusts that could support life.

Uranus "Ice Giant"

- The coldest planet, made of gas and ice
- Spins on its side, probably tipped over by a collision

CLOSE TO THE SUN

Although Mercury is closest to the sun and has more extreme temperature ranges than any other planet, it's not the planet with the highest temperatures in our solar system. The thick atmosphere on Venus, second closest to the sun, traps the sun's heat. This greenhouse effect means that Venus is the hottest planet.

Surface of Mercury

Mercury

Mercury is covered in craters. Many of these are named after famous artists, musicians, and writers, including children's author Dr. Seuss.

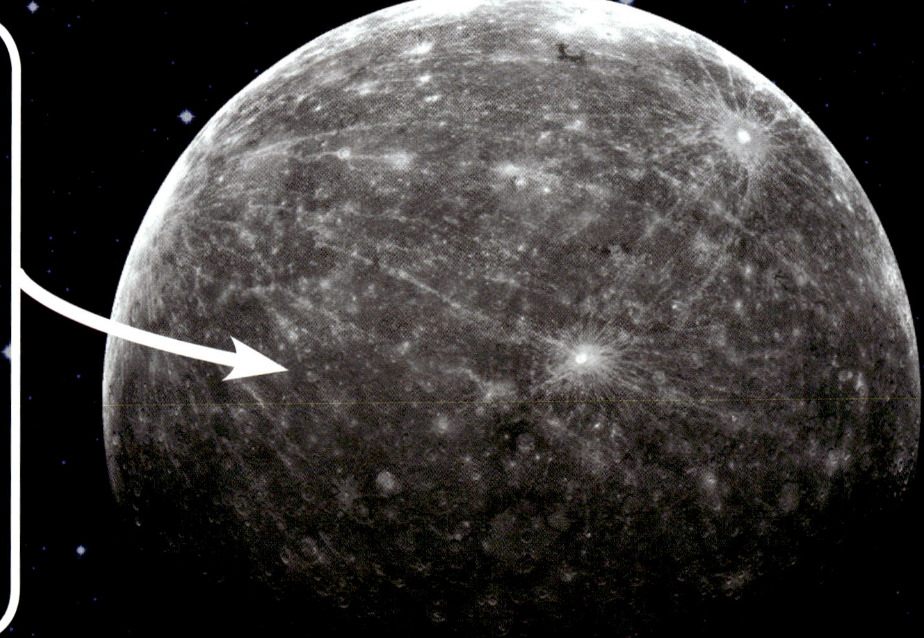

ROCKY FACTS

- Venus spins in the opposite direction of most planets.
- More than 40 spacecraft have explored Venus.
- The surface of Venus is hidden by clouds.
- Many scientists believe there was once water on the surface of Venus.
- Venus is named after the Roman goddess of love and beauty.

Alpha Region, Venus

OUR HOME

Earth is the only place we can be sure there is life of any kind. As far as we know, only humans on Earth are lucky enough to look up and see spectacular sights in the night sky. People have wondered about space since ancient times, but now we are learning to understand what we see.

AURORAS

At the poles, our atmosphere lights up with amazing curtains of light called auroras, flashing across the sky. They are caused by solar storms looping out from the sun and meeting the Earth's magnetic field. These natural light shows are called the northern or southern lights, depending on whether you are looking up in the Northern or Southern Hemisphere.

SOLAR ECLIPSE

When the sun, moon, and Earth line up across space, there is a solar eclipse. The moon blocks the sun's light and casts a shadow on Earth.

- Total solar eclipses can last up to eight and a half minutes and happen about every one and a half years.
- There are two other different types of solar eclipse: a partial eclipse and an annular eclipse.
- A lunar eclipse occurs when a full moon passes behind Earth into its shadow.

DID YOU KNOW?

Depending on the geometry of the sun, moon, and Earth, there can be between two and five solar eclipses each year.

MARS

Known as the "red planet" because of its blood-red, dusty surface, Mars is dry, rocky, and icy cold. It has the largest volcano in the solar system and polar ice caps. Like Earth, it rotates on a tilt so it has seasons too. Expeditions to Mars have discovered that, long ago, Mars was once much wetter and warmer and may even have hosted forms of life.

Life on Mars

Humans are making plans to live on Mars. It will be an exciting adventure, but Mars won't be a cozy, comfortable home. Unlike Earth, the atmosphere is mostly carbon dioxide, gravity is weak, and it's very cold indeed. So, astronauts will need to live inside a "habitat bubble" in which they can breathe, grow food, study space, and keep warm.

Sunset and sunrise

During the day

Red and blue sky

From the surface of Mars, the red dust makes the sky look brownish-red during the day. At sunset and sunrise, it's a cool blue around the sun.

MARS FACTS

- If the ground shudders on Mars, it might be a Marsquake.
- There are snow flurries on Mars, but not enough to build a snowman!

JUPITER

It's no secret that Jupiter is the largest planet in the solar system. But this description really doesn't do it justice. For one, the mass of Jupiter is 318 times as massive as the Earth. In fact, Jupiter is 2.5 times more massive than all of the other planets in the solar system combined.

Great Red Spot

The Great Red Spot on Jupiter is one of its most familiar features. This persistent anticyclonic storm, which is located to the south of its equator, is the most gigantic storm in the solar system.

Inside Jupiter ...

... there may be deep oceans of a strange metallic liquid that doesn't exist on Earth.

JUPITER FACTS

- The swirls and stripes on Jupiter's surface are cold, windy clouds of ammonia and water.
- Nine spacecraft have visited Jupiter.
- Jupiter does have rings, but they are too faint to see.
- Jupiter has a powerful magnetic field.

Spinning around

For all its size and mass, Jupiter moves quickly. In fact, the planet only takes about 10 hours to complete a full rotation on its axis. And, because Jupiter spins so rapidly, the planet has flattened out at the poles a little and bulges at its equator.

SATURN

Like Jupiter, Saturn is a gas planet so it doesn't have a solid surface. But below its swirling yellow clouds it has layers of unearthly liquids that may surround a rocky or even a liquid core.

Saturn's rings

There was a time when Saturn was without its rings. The latest findings suggest they formed during the age of the dinosaurs on Earth, 10 to 100 million years ago. The rings are made up of cosmic objects ranging from icy slivers to mountain-sized lumps. Sometimes, Saturn's rings are fully open and we see them in all their glory, but other times, when we see the rings edge on, it looks like they've disappeared.

Spinning around

Determining the rotation speed of Saturn was actually very difficult to do because the planet doesn't have a solid surface.

SATURN FACTS

- Saturn is so light that if you put this giant gas planet in water it would float.
- It has a unique polar jet stream with winds of 200 miles (322 km) per hour.
- It has only been visited four times by spacecraft.

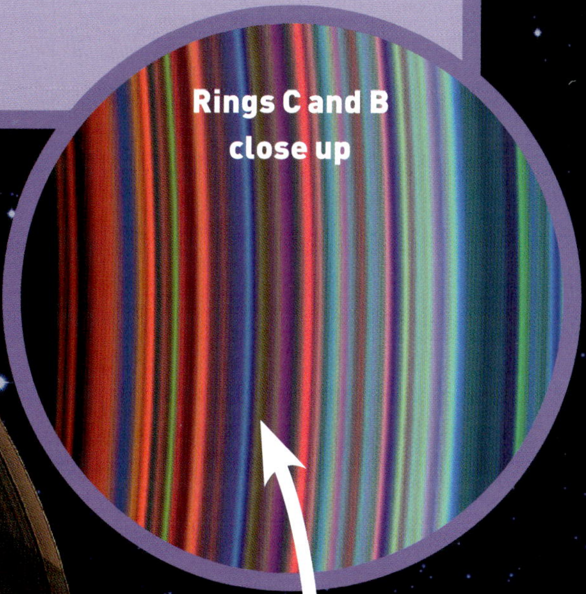

Rings C and B close up

The rings are named alphabetically in the order they were found. The main rings are A, B, and C.

ICE WORLDS

At the edge of the solar system are Uranus and Neptune, the most distant planets of all. These are known as the ice planets. Scientists believe that diamonds fall like raindrops toward the center of these ice-cold gas spheres, which spin so far away in dark space.

Uranus

Uranus is tipped over on its side. It is often described as rolling around the sun on its side. No other planet spins with such a tilt. It rotates the opposite way that Earth and most other planets do.

Neptune

Neptune is the furthest planet from the sun but strangely not the coldest. This is because there may be an ocean of superhot water beneath its clouds.

CHILLY FACTS

- The gas methane that swirls around both ice giants makes Uranus look blue-green and Neptune look darker blue, further from the sun.
- Neptune's clouds are whipped around by the strongest winds in the solar system.
- They are so far away that they have only been visited by one spacecraft, Voyager 2.

Clouds on Neptune

BELTS & CLOUDS

There are three astronomically big bands of rocks and ice in orbit in the solar system. Swept around by gravity, billions of different shapes and sizes of rock and ice form the asteroid belt, the Kuiper Belt, and probably the Oort Cloud, far out toward interstellar space.

ASTEROID BELT

- Most asteroids orbit the sun in the space between Mars and Jupiter.
- Space rocks in the asteroid belt are leftovers from the formation of the solar system.
- Ceres, the largest asteroid, is 295 miles (476 km) in diameter!
- The asteroid belt is 1 astronomical unit (AU) thick.

Ceres

KUIPER BELT

The Kuiper Belt is much bigger than the asteroid belt and lies at the outer edges of the solar system. It's thought to stretch across 20 AU of space. It is also made up of space rocks of all sizes in a region beyond Neptune. There are estimated to be trillions of comets in the Kuiper Belt.

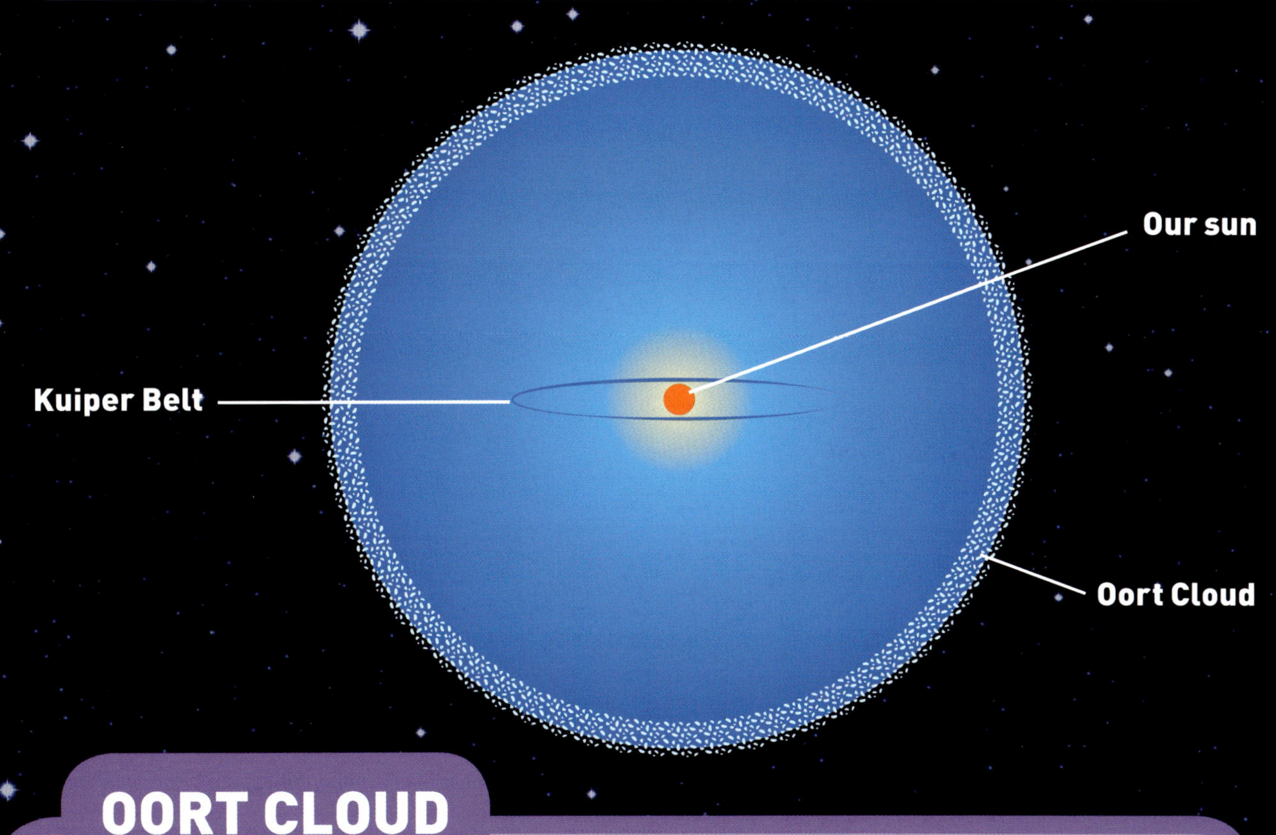

OORT CLOUD

No one has ever seen it, but scientists believe that the Oort Cloud exists. This shell of icy objects, like comets, is believed to lie about 2,000 AU from the sun in the outermost reaches of the solar system. There may be more than a trillion objects spinning in the Oort Cloud.

FOCUS ON SPACE ROCKS

WHAT IS AN ASTEROID?

It's a small, rocky object orbiting the sun. Some are dwarf planets while others are just chunky space rocks.

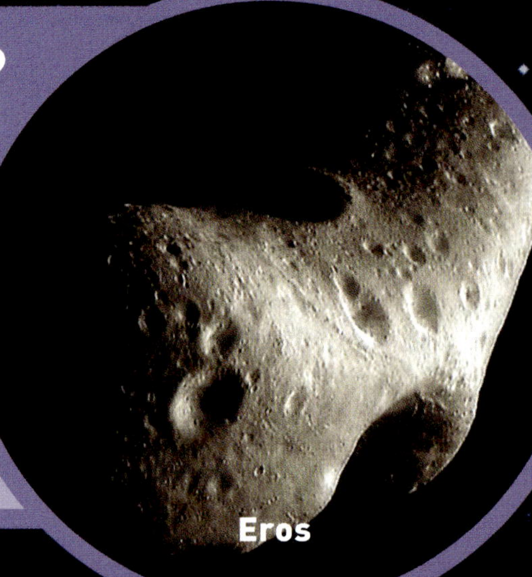
Eros

WHAT IS A COMET?

It's a small cosmic object made up from ice and dust. When comets orbit close to the sun, ice melts and a white "tail" of gas and dust streams away from the object. There are over 3,500 known comets, some as big as a small town!

METEOROID, METEOR, OR METEORITE?

- A meteoroid is a bit of rock that may be part of a comet or asteroid traveling through outer space.
- A meteor is the streak of light you see when a meteoroid zooms through Earth's atmosphere and burns up. Most disintegrate and break up, but some reach Earth.
- A meteorite is a lump of space rock that crashes into Earth. Less than 5 percent of meteorites reach the ground. But if you find a small, shiny, fist-sized rock somewhere, it might just be part of a meteorite.

A giant meteor

DID YOU KNOW?

Around the time life first formed on Earth, there was a heavy bombardment of meteorites smashing into the planet. They formed what are now some of the oldest rocks on Earth.

CAN I SEE IT?

WITH YOUR NAKED EYE

You can see much of the solar system with your own eyes. If you know when and where to look in the night sky, on a clear night you can easily find the five brightest planets: Mercury, Venus, Mars, Jupiter, and Saturn.

- You can only see one moon with your naked eye: Earth's moon.
- Neptune is the only planet that you can't ever see with your naked eye.
- You can see stars in the Milky Way in interstellar space, and even spot the galaxy Andromeda as a white smudge in the distant sky.
- You can glimpse the bright flash of the International Space Station whizzing by if you know when to look.

WITH YOUR BINOCULARS

You can get a much closer look at planets, and even other galaxies, through binoculars. You can explore craters on the moon and even spot the four Galilean moons of Jupiter.

WITH YOUR TELESCOPE

You can see the ice giants Neptune and Uranus and even focus in on a distant comet or an asteroid with a telescope.

WHAT IS A TELESCOPE?

A telescope is a magnification tool. Using one is the best way to investigate the sky because it will allow you to see distant objects more clearly. With the most gigantic, very powerful telescopes, space agencies spot distant galaxies in deep space and take amazing pictures.

GLOSSARY

astronomical unit (AU) a unit equal to the distance of Earth from the sun, about 93 million miles (150 million km)

atmosphere the mixture of gases that surround a planet

axis an imaginary straight line around which a planet turns

cosmic having to do with outer space or the universe

equator an imaginary line around a planet that is the same distance from its north and south poles

hemisphere one half of a planet

magnetic field the area near a planet where magnetic forces can be found

Milky Way the galaxy in which Earth is found

orbit to travel in a circle or oval around something, or the path used to make that trip

rotate to turn around a fixed point

tilt the state of having one side higher than another

volcano an opening in a planet's surface through which hot, liquid rock sometimes flows

FOR MORE INFORMATION

BOOKS

Beer, Julie, and Stephanie Warren Drimmer. *Can't Get Enough Space Stuff*. Washington, DC: National Geographic, 2022.

Ring, Susan. *Dwarf Planets*. New York, NY: AV2, 2021.

Wilberforce, Bert. *The Planets*. New York, NY: Gareth Stevens Publishing, 2021.

WEBSITES

www.ducksters.com/science/physics/space_exploration_timeline.php
Use this timeline to mark when different parts of the solar system were discovered and explored.

www.planetsforkids.org/
Read more about each planet, and other cosmic bodies, on this website.

spaceplace.nasa.gov/menu/solar-system/
Check out NASA's website for kids that tells all about the solar system.

Publisher's note to educators and parents: Our editors have carefully reviewed these websites to ensure that they are suitable for students. Many websites change frequently, however, and we cannot guarantee that a site's future contents will continue to meet our high standards of quality and educational value. Be advised that students should be closely supervised whenever they access the internet.

INDEX